I

A Handbook for Masonic Initiation.

Amor Russell
Copyright © 2020

Amor Russell is a Gnostic Christian Mystic and Freemason. His philosophical studies of the ancient mystery schools is the platform of his entire teaching, as he openly proclaims the Illumined Gospel of Self-Revelation to all mankind.

This little book is for the purpose of Masonic Education and Greater Light and is to be shared with every Brother and Sister within the Lodge.

amorrussell.ananda@gmail.com

This small booklet is a perfect handbook to give out to anyone who has recently become a Mason. It is an edited and expanded version of the first 2 chapters of my previous book "Know thyself", *only within these pages, the topic and symbolism are based on Masonic Initiation and the Mystical Ascent alone.* I made this little book specifically for members of the Lodge that are interested in the esoterica of spiritual Freemasonry. If you are a Freemason, then these writings are a valuable tool for more Masonic education and Spiritual Light.

Amor Russell

Table of Contents

Introduction

All the principles herein are based on a single truth. Knowledge of this truth is innate in everyone, but not until it is found and brought forth into our consciousness is it fully realized and accepted. Hence, the portals of the ancient mystery schools bore the saying, Man, Know Thy Self or as Jesus said, "Seek first the kingdom of God which is within you. He who attains this knowledge has found the key that unlocks the door to everything.

All the great mystery traditions tell us that the lower self must be submitted to the higher self, and the higher self will then realize its oneness with God. In every true mystery school this process is accomplished by only three stages or Degrees. Through spiritual consciousness alone is this seen and known. Illumination comes only from the higher mind and its vision. In other words, as your higher Soul-consciousness gradually develops through study and meditation, it leads your mind in alignment with new creation realities, where nothing is impossible and everything you need is already supplied.

On the Initiatic path, you will practice the necessary spiritual principles that truly benefit you on your inward journey. Illumination on the mystical path is the way of entering the Divine Wisdom of the God Self within. This Divine Wisdom is called Gnosis [knowledge in Greek] by the Illumined Mystics. Here, you will come to experience the intimacy of the all-inclusive Divine presence, dwelling at the shrine of your very own inner being.

The goal of all mystical processes is the purification of the natural human being- that is, the extraction of the pure gold of your spiritual essence from the husk of the outer personality (the ego). The final objective of all this is the purification of the lower faculties and the realization of an elevated state of consciousness, wherein consciousness enters into a union with the higher mind and ultimately with the universal mind.

The final step is when our conscious mind is absorbed in the omnipresent Light- when the Divine Spirit and our Spirit are finally recognized as the One Spirit. As water poured into water, or milk poured into milk, our Spirit merges with the Spirit of God. As Light transfers to Light, the individual and the universal become One- this is the alchemical marriage.

"Among most of the Ancient Nations there was, in addition to their public worship, a private one styled the Mysteries; to which those only were admitted who had been prepared by certain ceremonies called initiations... Masonry is identical with the Ancient Mysteries..." (Morals and Dogma, 1871)

Albert Pike

Masonic writer of the 1800s

Part 1

The Ancient Mysteries

The ancient mystery schools of wisdom had neither silver nor gold to give; neither name nor fame. What they had to offer was spiritual Illumination- the Christed consciousness which would lead the aspirant into harmony, joy, peace, and glory, but not always in the way that he might imagine or outline. In such a school, Initiation, which was a significant landmark on the spiritual journey, always took the candidate from material sense to spiritual consciousness; and while the method of study, practice, and unfoldment might differ from place to place, and from one era to another, the goal and the result were always the same. Self-knowledge was always the supreme aim of attainment.

Initiation means rebirth, or to unfold into something totally new. It is the beginning of a new outlook on life, with a new set of faculties; a passage into a new type of existence. The characteristics of this event are marked by an expansion of consciousness, to include an awareness of higher levels of existence.

Initiation represents spiritual regeneration- the activation of enlightened vision, committed to an entirely new set of principles than those of mundane human existence. Initiation is the realization and attainment of immortality itself. It is awakening to another dimension entirely. In the most ancient mystery schools, the seeker of knowledge was born again and received a new name. He was fully Christed. He had been awakened spiritually. Through the mysteries of the Spirit he now declared, "I am the Resurrection and the Life. He Who believes in Me will live, even though He has died" (John 11:25). If we comprehend these ancient mystery schools in all their depth, we will understand the very essence of both Esoteric Freemasonry and Mystic Christianity.

All humanity can be divided into two principle groupings in respect to their spiritual development. The first, and by far the smallest in number, is comprised of those who have entered into the deeper mysteries of life that lead to Illumination, or Initiation.

The other group embraces the masses of mankind who have not attained to this stage of development. They are nourished in the same Mysteries as are those more advanced, but are not yet able to apprehend them except as they are presented in parable, allegory, rituals and ceremonies. Only as an individual develops the spiritual vision and understanding to penetrate beneath the surface of these external representations does he or she become qualified and worthy, to be taught the deeper mysteries by means of Initiation.

And so, since the beginning of recorded time, all the great religions have been founded on Initiation. This accounts for the similarity in all basic teachings of ritualistic practices of all the great religious traditions. The ceremonials performed in the temples of old were designed for taking the three successive steps or degrees of spiritual attainment leading to Mastership.

The first recorded Initiations that took place occurred in the caves if India. In Masonry's most magnificent treatise, Albert Pikes Morals and Dogma, he writes of these early Indian traditions: "The Indian Mysteries were celebrated in subterranean caverns and grottos hewn in the solid rock; and the Initiates adored the Deity, symbolized by the solar fire. The candidate, long wandering in darkness, truly wanted Light, and the worship taught him was the worship of God, the Source of Light."

Following the attainment of Initiation, the successful candidate addressed himself exultingly in praise and adoration to the Supreme God of Light. A vow was then taken to forever thereafter allow the Illumined Soul control over the outer form, to be devoted to his superiors, to keep his body pure, to govern his tongue, and to observe a passive obedience in receiving the secret doctrines. He was then sprinkled with water, certain magic words were whispered in his ear, his shoes were removed from his feet, and finally he encircled the temple floor three times.

All initiatory ceremonialism is formulated in accord with the three aspects of Divinity. Christianity knows the Divine Trinity, Father, Son and Holy Spirit. In India the Trinity comprises Brahma, Vishnu, and Shiva; in Egypt, Osiris, Isis and Horus. Corresponding Trinities can be found in all the major world religions. These three aspects of Divinity correlate to three principle laws of nature, known as Creation, Preservation and Transformation.

Again, these three divine aspects and their manifestation in nature are represented in the Masonic Lodge in the three offices of the Master, Junior Warden and the Senior Warden. God the Father and Creator of heaven and earth is represented by the Master, the Son, the Preserver and Giver, by the Junior Warden; and the Holy Spirit, the Comforter and Enlightener, by the Senior Warden who effects the necessary evolutionary transformation.

Masonry, being founded on the universal truths belonging to Initiation, recognizes the one Source whence has come spiritual Light for the guidance of all people. This Light has found various expressions in the several sacred scriptures of the world. These several revelations have been adapted to the people to whom they were given and were in accordance of the time of their release. Hence, Masonry places on the Alter of its Lodges the Bible of the pervading religion of the land in which the Lodge is located. The supreme tenet in which all Masons ascribe is a belief in God.

Theological differences are left to the individual's own interpretation. The principles of which Mystic Masonry are founded are, therefore, wide as the world and as all-inclusive as humanity itself.

The teachings of Mystic Masonry are founded on the Ancient Mysteries. However, modern English Masonry in its present form had its beginning in London about the year 1725. Modern Masonry is nothing more or less than a good old boys club focused on community service. Mystic Masonry, on the other hand, had its inception in the initiatory schools of Ancient Egypt which itself evolved from the most Ancient Mystery Temples of Atlantis. The key words in Modern Masonry is Fraternity and Sociability. The key ideal of Mystic Masonry is spiritual illumination through Initiation. It is Mystic Masonry that this book is concerned and not the social Lodges of mainstream English Freemasonry.

The Three Degrees of Initiation

Initiation is the acknowledgment and completion of a great work. A true Initiation is an experience into a higher state of being. The true Initiation is always divided into three steps or "degrees" These three steps can be found in every authentic spiritual rite, order, practice, and religion, including Freemasonry. This is because these three degrees or steps correspond to the three fundamental actions of Nature: Affirming, Denying, and Reconciling. Regeneration, or initiation, is directly related to the Third Force or Action of all manifestation in Nature, which is the Reconciliation of Spirit (active energy) and Matter (passive energy); as this action gives birth to the new man of the Third Degree of the Ancient Mysteries.

The three steps of Initiation into the Ancient Mysteries can be summarized as follows: First a person must undergo a purification process. This means cleansing all of their inner qualities: physical, mental, emotional, and spiritual. This stage also represents mastery of the physical plane and is the work of the apprentice.

Second, the person must learn to discipline and strengthen his or her mind, for only by cleansing our thoughts, do we find inner peace. This stage represents mastery of the mental and emotional. Third, the person must give the ultimate sacrifice. In order to be completely united with the Divine, one must crucify their false self by surrendering their personal will and past life completely. Only then are we worthy of entrance into the celestial Lodge on High.

A true Initiation is the elevation of consciousness from bodily perception to something more Divine. It is for this reason that the famous ancient Greek Philosopher and Initiate, Plato, once quoted his teacher, Socrates as saying, "Our Mysteries have a very real meaning. He that has been purified and initiated will dwell with the Gods". To become Initiated in the first Degree means to be reborn, the new birth into a higher phase of life, were the human consciousness becomes a servant of his spiritual will. When a candidate is passed in the second Degree, he leaves behind the egoic world and is born into a life of the Spirit. In the final Degree he sets his vision towards the east, where he discovers the Blazing Star, typifying the Christ Light, and also the star which guided the wise men to the manger where they found the holy babe, which is allegorically our true Self- our Divine Spark.

The Necessity of Developing Inner Vision

The mantra of the Ancient Mysteries was this: "Look within and Know Thyself, for your salvation is now. Time is an illusion. Awaken to the vision of Spirit and be reborn today." This is also the voice of the enlightened Mind of Christ, longing to be revealed within you. Christ is risen from the sepulcher of your own consciousness when you behold Him in the Light of spiritual vision. To be crucified, buried, risen and then Christed, is the true message of all Initiatic mystery traditions.

In the ancient mystery schools, true spirituality is understood to be a unique series of rituals that welcome the Divinities and build a strong relationship with Them, so that we can ascend to Their realm. Initiation was established in order to activate different centers of power within the Initiate, and to open their perception to the invisible world. Upon entrance into the mystery schools the instruction says, "The way of Illumination now stands open before you. Look well within yourself and may the Light of Divine understanding guide you."

The Mystic life is about transcending duality through the reconciliation of opposites, and awakening your spiritual Eye. The only way to experience the God seeing Self, is to recognize the divinity in everyone you meet and to see them healed, whole, and perfect. Here is the key to Illumination according to the mystical teachings of Christ: "The Light of the body is the Eye. If therefore thine Eye be single (non-dual vision), the whole body (physical, mental and spiritual) shall be filled with Light (joy, peace and radiance)" (Matthew 6:22 of the Bible).

We may see each other as being individual in physical appearance, and as being different in human personality, yet once awakened, we no longer see others as being different or separate in our spiritual identity. We are all One Spirit, just as the Moon reflects the same Light in several ponds, so the universal consciousness reflects one consciousness in all its individual expressions. Such a "God seeing vision" is to recognize the One awareness that looks through all eyes, beyond the many forms. And once you see everyone beyond all appearances, you are seeing with the eyes of Christ, and you are seeing everyone as God sees you. "We shall be like Him, because we shall see Him as He is" (1 John 3:2 of the Bible).

The Goal of Initiation

The spiritual life is the way of self-transcendence and not just self-improvement. It is not ultimately about perfecting the ego personality; it is about awakening from the dream of personality altogether. Divine vision awakens the higher Self, "the true Light, which guides every man coming into the world" (John 1:9). "Christ in you, the hope of glory" (Colossians 1:27) is our true Self. The birth of the Illumined Christ in you is the opening of the inner realms of singular consciousness. The awakening of a higher set of faculties, when activated, will take over your entire being.

Symbolism: The Ancient Mystery Language

Masonic teachings are communicated by means of mystic symbols, emblems and allegories, which is the language of the Ancient Mysteries. When we learn to interpret this language, the deepest truths open up to us. If we do not learn to interpret it then the deepest secrets remain closed. Symbols and allegories both conceal and reveal simultaneously. They conceal their secrets from those who have failed to prove themselves worthy of receiving them, yet they reveal those same secrets to those who have proved themselves to be ready. St. Paul made this clear when he said, "Milk is for babies while meat is for strong men" (Hebrews 5:13-14; 1 Corinthians 3:2 of the Bible).

Albert Pike a foremost Sage of Freemasonry, states that the Lodge teaches morality by means of its symbolism, and much more. It is this much more, this deeper teaching to which Pike refers, that is the main focus of this text and is the heart of esoteric Masonry.

Masonic ritual is the most magnificent symbolism to be found in our modern world age. The Rites, remnants of the Ancient Mysteries, show us the complete way to spiritual Illumination. Unfortunately, however few today in the Lodges of America known little if anything about it or have any conception of the glorious truths on which its work is founded. All Masons are enjoined to become the "Sons of Light".

In the first Degree the candidate comes, poor, naked and blind, in search of Light. The number is the most important number associated with the first Degree, and it means complete devotion or dedication, body, mind and Spirit. Three principle officers conduct this Degree, in which there are three Greater Lights and thee lesser Lights, all representing our higher and lower facilities. Admittance into the Lodge room is gained after three knocks at the door, and there are three journeyings around the room in quest for Light. These are just a few uses of the number three in the first Degree which we will go more in detail in the next chapter.

What is True Mystic Masonry?

Many who are against Freemasonry are religious fundamentalists, and subsequently are also against every religion that is not their own. And even among their own, they are divided over who has the right interpretations of their particular religious book. Meanwhile, the Mystic Mason does not buy into any of this nonsense. The Mystic Mason renounces religious intolerance, and can worship God at any shrine, temple, or altar in the world. It makes no difference if it is a Christian, Hindu, Jewish, or Muslim sacred space. For the Mystic Mason, all paths universally lead to the One, Omnipresent, Godhead, or Universal Oversoul.

People can say what they want about the political conspiracies associated with the history of Masonry, (and indeed may be true as far as apostate masons are concerned), however, pure Masonic Initiates (the Mystics of the Lodge) have no interest in political agendas. Esoteric Masonry and the mystics of the Lodge have always been about overcoming their lower passions, transcending the duality within themselves, and awakening to their higher Self.

Any agenda or political conspiracy associated with Freemasonry would actually be anti-Masonry, and totally against every moral precept and spiritual principles of our Masonic oaths- which is to be in service to all mankind and do them no harm.

As far as dark conspiracies are concerned, there is no question that such things exist in world history, even to this present day. The same dark side of history could apply to the Christian and Muslim empires as well. In truth, every organization has a shadow side. Nevertheless, Esoteric spirituality remains a true path to enlightenment, whether it be Esoteric Buddhism, Sufism, Hinduism, Freemasonry or Christianity. If any deception is going on within any such group, it is only because they have chosen to dishonor the moral principles of their Craft.

What is true Masonry really about? Do you really want to know the hidden mysteries of Freemasonry? Below are several quotes from my own collection of esoteric books by Masonic mystics.

Hear ye them.

"There are all manner of reasons why people seek to achieve an elevated level of consciousness. Some want to be able to read other people's minds and learn secret things for their own advantage. Others want to be able to perform magic and impose their will on the universe. From the Masonic point of view there is only one reason for seeking to rise in consciousness; and that is to reach the Middle Chamber of one's Soul and ultimately, to experience the Divine Presence." W. Kirk Macnulty

"As that great authority and initiate of the mysteries, Paul, taught, we can only attain to the Master's resurrection by "being made conformable unto His death," and we "must die with Him if we are to be raised like Him': The three year ministry of the Christian Master ended with His death and, these refer to the three Degrees of the Craft which also end in the mystical death of the Masonic candidate - and his subsequent raising or resurrection." W.L. Wilmshurst

"Being made a Mason symbolizes the birth of Christ within, and before anyone can attain this mystical rebirth, he must have progressed some way along the road of evolution, have gained certain experiences, and learnt certain lessons. To use modern language, the second Degree teaches of the birth of the Christ Spirit within us, while the third indicates that mystically we, like the great Master, must die and rise again. As Saint. Paul says, " Die daily in Christ." J.S. Ward

"In the Third Degree we rise into the consciousness where there is no health and there is no wealth. There is neither good nor bad; there is neither virtue nor vice; there is neither honor or dishonor; there is only a spiritual state of being which is described as "My kingdom," the Christ-consciousness. When we come to the third stage, which is reached by passing through a series of Initiations, each marking a transition from a lower state of consciousness to a higher one, there is no sowing and there is no reaping: there is only a state of Divine being which, when attained, enables us to live by Grace. When the Son of God is raised up in us and is alive, we need take no thought, for It does all things for us." Joel S. Goldsmith

"The process whereby a man may so perfect, purify and ripen his own consciousness, that he may have the same direct awareness of his immortal part that was attained by our ancient brethren, are the real secrets of Freemasonry. They are indicated with sufficient details and clearness in the rites and symbols of the Craft Lodge Degrees. Not for nothing is the highest of these called the sublime Degree of Master Mason. Not for nothing is the legend of this Degree concerned with a disillusion and a raising. For the old forms through which the serpent force expresses itself must be killed out before they may be raised to a new life." Paul Foster Chase

"The true Mason is not creed-bound. He realizes with the Divine Illumination of his Lodge, that as a Mason his religion must be universal: Christ, Buddha or Mohammed, the name means little, for he recognizes only the Light and not the bearer. He worships at every shrine, bows before every altar, whether in temple, mosque or cathedral, realizing with his truer understanding the oneness of all spiritual truth." Manly P. Hall

"Masonry preaches no new religion; it but reiterates the Commandment announced by Jesus, which also was announced by every great reformer or religion since history began. Drop the theological barnacles from the religion of Jesus, as taught by him, and by the Essenes and Gnostics of the first centuries, and it becomes the mysticism of Masonry." C.H. Vail

"Whatever we may think of Jesus of Nazareth as a manifestation of the Logos, it is with the indwelling Christ in our own hearts that we have to do, in the working out of our salvation. For the Divine man, the Higher Self, is the Christ. This was taught in the schools of Initiation ages before the Church limited the Divine manifestation to one particular man. It is the esoteric teaching of the Divine nature of man". - William Kingsland

"The real Initiation is an internal, not an external process. To transform means to regenerate, and this comes by trial, by effort, by self-conquest, by sorrow, disappointment, failure, and daily renewal of the conflict. It is thus man must work out his own salvation. The consummation of Initiation is the finding of the Christos." Reuben Swinburne Clmer

"Every Soul must "work out its own salvation" and "take the Kingdom of Heaven by force." Salvation by faith and the vicarious atonement were not taught, as now interpreted, by Jesus, nor are these doctrines taught in the exoteric Scriptures. They are later and ignorant perversions of the original doctrines. In the early Church, as in the Secret Doctrine, there was not one Christ for the whole world, but a potential Christ in every man. Theologians first made a fetish of the Impersonal, Omnipresent Divinity; and then tore the Christos from the hearts of all humanity in order to deify Jesus; that they might have a God-man peculiarly their own." J.D. Buck

"The Third Master's Degree has been called the "Accolade of Masonry," for a candidate passing through this Rite should have earned the powers and abilities of true mastership. A candidate in the Master's Degree is permitted to use all the tools of the two previous Degrees plus an additional one, the trowel, symbolic of the cohesive power of love, for mastership can be achieved only as love becomes the motivation of the candidate's every thought, word and act." Corrinnee Heline

"Ever since mankind, the prodigal spirit sons of our Father in Heaven, wandered into the wilderness of the world and fed upon the husks of its pleasures, which starve the body, there has been within man's heart a soundless voice urging him to return; but most men are so engrossed in material interests that they hear it not. The Mystic Mason who has heard this inner voice feels impelled by an inner urge to seek for the Lost Word; to build a house of God, a temple of the spirit, where he may meet the Father face to face and answer His call." - Max Hendel

As anyone can see from the writings above, true spiritual Freemasonry, is not anything evil and has nothing to do with political conspiracies whatsoever. Mystic Masonry is an ego transcending process of Illumination through Initiation. The Great Work of Mystic Masonry is devoted especially and directly to Emotional and Spiritual development, to the awakening of the Godly love nature, the Divine Spark or Christos, which must become the conscious Soul or Christic Self.

The Masonic Way of Christification

Is Christianity and Freemasonry compatible? The answer is "No," at least not on an exoteric level. However, on an esoteric level the answer is "Yes." In fact, Freemasonry is compatible with all the worlds great spiritual and religious traditions on an esoteric level. *Let us now consider the Masonic Christ.*

In every Masonic Lodge two moveable pillars are employed as part of the regular furniture, Boaz representing the heart and Jachin representing the head, and at appropriate parts of the Initiation the Candidate is placed between them to signify that the two opposed principles (love and wisdom) must be equilibrated in himself. Few Lodges, however, possess such pillars or understanding of their meaning; hence the need for instruction stands at the very threshold of Masonic science, just as the pillars themselves stood at the entrance to King Solomon's symbolic temple. 'I come from between the pillars' is a saying by the Candidate in Egyptian rituals far older than Solomon's Temple, and it signified

'I have trodden the narrow way and balanced the light and darkness in myself'. In the great Initiation Hall of the temple at Delphi there are said to be the pediments of two stone pillars between which, authorities have suggested, the Candidate had to stand and pass through. They are so close together that in standing between them he touched both, uniting them as it were in his own person, as to squeeze through them was a matter of effort and difficulty. **Hence the references elsewhere to 'the narrow way', to 'passing through the eye of a needle' and to 'the street which is called Straight,' (Acts 9; 11).**

The Mystical accent of Christian Mysticism is indeed experienced within the alchemy of Masonry. The symbol of the Cross, carries the same meaning as the two pillars (Jachin and Boaz) in Masonry, only in the Lodge they are presented as two upright columns. | | They are prominent in all Degree work. Put very simply, the vertical beam of the cross represents masculine energy, and the horizontal beam represents feminine energy. It is the union, or "crossing" of these two opposite forces in nature that gives birth to the indwelling Christ.

The goal of all Degree work is to awaken this Christ principle and bring it into fuller manifestation. This is why every candidate is called a "widow's son," until his head and his heart is brought into equilibrium- a harmonious blending of the masculine and feminine forces of Spirit within himself.

As the Christ said: "When you make male and female into a single one, so that the male shall not be male, and the female shall not be female . . . then you will enter the kingdom of heaven," (the gospel of Thomas). Jesus is not speaking of transgenderism, or gender confusion on the physical plane. He is speaking of active and passive spiritual forces that are found only within our being. The masculine active- fire, and feminine passive- water, (also known in psychology as the right and left hemispheres of the brain.)

John 3:3 "Very truly I tell you, no one can enter the kingdom of God unless they are born of WATER and the SPIRIT." These are symbolized in Freemasonry by the two pillars of the first and second Degree as Boaz (Water) and Jachin (Fire or Spirit).

The Lion's Paw is a very important part of Initiation. This grip is a reference to the Lion of the Tribe of Judah, "The Cosmic Christ whose symbol is the Sun." The initiate is introduced to the Lion's Paw in the Master Mason Degree during the portrayal of the Hiramic legend which is symbolic of spiritual resurrection and immortality. The symbolism of resurrection is an important part of the quest for Mystic union with Deity. In moving from darkness to Light, the candidate is spiritually reborn in the Third Degree. From the hand of a trusted Brother, one is raised to a higher level of consciousness and being.

The First Stage – Purgation

During this Degree, we cleanse ourselves of negative thoughts and surrender our lower desire nature. The body is TRANCENDED through fasting, vigil and prayer. The purpose of this stage is that the new Christed mystic may grow detached from worldly things and thus achieve what is referred to as dispassion. In the pattern of the Tabernacle, the first section, the outer court, contained the alter whereon the bodies of sacrificial animals were burned. This ceremony symbolized the cleansing of our animal passions. In the New Testament, it is demonstrated as Jesus hanging on the cross, which is a universal symbol of sacrificial love, and points to the sacrifice of our own carnal self. In Freemasonry it the Degree of the Entered Apprentice.

The Second Stage – Illumination

During this Degree, we become conscious of the Presence of God, and the Soul is Illumined by the Light of spiritual vision. The practice of contemplative meditation and prayer is intensified as the outer man moves to the background and the inner man begins to be revealed. In the second or inner court of the Tabernacle the fires of the alter are fed only with the purest olive oil, symbolizing the Holy Spirits presence within our Illumined consciousness. In the New Testament pattern, it is demonstrated by the material stone being rolled away from the tomb of Christ. In Freemasonry it is the Degree of the Fellow Craft.

The Third Stage – Mystical Union

During this Degree, the Soul finds rest through inner silence. The spinal Spirit Fire is lifted from the throat to the top of the head. This is the crowning attainment of the great work. Likewise, in the third or high court of the Tabernacle is placed the Holy of Holies. When this sacred fire touches the head center we are brought into this sacred space, and are given the keys to the kingdom of heaven. This is the Degree of glorification. And is alluded to in the New Testament as the Resurrection of Christ. It is the Mystic Marriage between man and God, as our heaven and our earth become one. In Freemasonry it is experienced as the final Degree of Mastership or Master Mason.

Born of Water and Spirit

Everything said about Jesus in the bible, contains the allegorical keys to spiritual Illumination or Initiation. To become Christed or Initiated in His name, is to be spiritually Illumined by the Divine Presence. "Many are called but few are chosen" The way is open to come and partake of the waters of life freely.

Few heeds the call of the higher life, and of these only rare Souls succeed in lifting the veil of mortal perception and passing into the Holy of Hollies, beyond the world of flesh, and finally released into wider realms of love and service.

The Christ said: "If you are not born of the Water and the Spirit you will not know the kingdom of God." In esoteric science, water has always been considered the passive element and Spirit the active principle. If you are not born of Water and Spirit: that is to say you must be Initiated by the purification and Illumination both the conscious (active) and subconscious (passive) aspects of mind.

The Christ likened the kingdom to a grain of mustard seed, which when sown in the earth brings forth much fruit. "By their fruits you shall know them" The power of the Christ-life that is within the seed causes it to push its way up through the darkness until at last the tender plant breaks through the earth and finds the Sunlight. In likewise manner are those who are Initiated, Illumined and Perfected in their Spirit.

The work of Initiation is concerned with the awakening of the duel force. Its control and finally its transmutation. The Father aspect (Fire) and the Mother aspect (Water) are within man. By the activity of the Holy Spirit, the Son of Light is Born. This is the Light that shineth in darkness (materiality) and the darkness comprehend it not. By awakening the Christ within, man lifts himself above and beyond all personal limitations into a consciousness of peace, harmony and plenty. He then realizes a new life where there is, no more sorrow', no more tears, no more death, for the former things have passed away and his spiritual facilities have been renewed."

The Way Crossification.

To discover Christianity's deeper mysteries of esoteric wisdom, we need only to look at the symbol of Christ crucified between two thieves, both with opposite natures, with Christ in the center. This is an allusion to the three pillars of alchemy- body, mind, and spirit, which must be crucified through the process of Initiation, for the new being to emerge.

The alchemical number 3 represents the union of polar opposites (the two thieves) which are experienced in the 1st and 2nd Degree- symbolized by the two pillars in the temple. Our true Self is seen as the 3rd pillar at the center, who is spiritually risen in the 3rd Degree. As seen in nature the union of opposites (masculine and feminine,) gives birth to a third force. This rule of three is seen everywhere in Masonic and Christian symbolism, as well as in the world of biology. It is symbolic of spiritual perfection. It completes the triangle and is the final Degree in the alchemical laboratory of blue Lodge Masonry.

According to esoteric Christianity, the crucifixion is a parable, an allegory that describes the process of Initiation. There are two thieves hanging on each side of the crucified Christ. The crucified Christ in you, also hangs between these same allegorical thieves. In Masonry these thieves are the two pillars of the Lodge, which are symbolic of the body and mind. When they are undisciplined and left to their own delusions, they become thieves, robbing us of our own Christhood, which is crucified on the cross of matter.

Freemasonry, just like the Christic mysteries, deals with the tripartite nature of man, physical, mental, spiritual, (in that order,) by means of the three Degrees. The purification of our physical actions and mental thoughts leads us to the final stage of enlightenment. This is the way of Initiation in all mystery schools.

The Crucifixion takes place on the cross of our human experience. Christ, (which is our true spiritual will,) is crucified between the two thieves of our fallen physical and mental natures. According to the mysteries; they must all three be crucified before any resurrection is possible. To the body we decree, "I need do nothing". To the mind we say "Be still and know". And to our will we let go and say "Not my will but thine will be done".

Another Masonic interpretation is that the two thieves represent the unenlightened condition of mankind. They are identified with the first two Degrees of Masonic Initiation. The thief on the left represents our fallen physical nature that clings to bodily survival. The other thief is our fallen mental nature, which desires only to be in heaven with Christ today.

When these two thieves, (our fallen physical and mental natures,) are crucified and Christed through the process of Initiation, the eternal Christ in you is taken off the cross, were he resurrects from the empty tomb of mortal existence.

The Allegorical Crucifixion

The Christian cross represents the point of intersection between the earthly (horizontal) and heavenly (vertical) planes of experience. The Initiatic Path of the cross symbolizes the path of the kundalini fire as it rises from the base of the spine to the head. The Christ on the cross signifies the Spirit within man whose ultimate goal is to become a fully Christed one. Everyone born into the world is a crucified Christ on the cross of mortal existence, until they are resurrected by the spiritual birth of their true Divine nature

Part 2

The Masonic Path of Initiation.

In Freemasonry, and all other ancient mystery schools including Mystic Christianity, the great process of Illumination is revealed through the first, second and third Degrees of Initiation. The word Degree, in its primitive meaning, signifies a step. The Degrees of Freemasonry are, then, the steps by which the candidate ascends from a lower to a higher level of consciousness. These are, "Entered Apprentice," "Fellow Craft," and "Master Mason," in that order.

Every Masonic Lodge is an alchemical laboratory, whereby the candidate goes through the first three stages of alchemical transmutation: Calcination, Dissolution, Separation. The entire process of Initiation is one of regeneration. It means developing your inner most essence and awakening spiritually, first to birth and then to full maturity. This involves a mystical death to the lower principles that obstruct our growth.

To become an Initiate means to be reborn, the second birth into a new and higher phase of life. When a candidate is Initiated, he or she leaves behind them the claims of the outer world and is born into a new life in the Spirit. This new life entails much painful preparation, sacrifice and purification. These are typified in the Masonic apron made of lambs wool, the lamb being the symbol of purity, sacrifice and transmutation. The apron is formed of a square and a triangle, their combined sides adding up to the number seven, and the significance of the number seven is the completion of the spiritual quest.

Perhaps the most familiar symbols of Masonry are the Square and the Compass resting on an open bible. These are the three Greater Lights of the Lodge, symbolic of the Illumined Soul faculties. For a Mystic Mason this arrangement is profound indeed. In the Apprentice Degree the candidate is instructed to use the Square for aligning his or her life with the Golden Rule; the Compass, to circumscribe desire and keep passion within due bounds.

Esoterically, the Square represents the feminine principle (the heart) and the Compass, the masculine principle (the mind); while the Bible, the supreme textbook of life, teaches the aspirant how to attain equilibrium between the two (head and heart). Polarity – a complete blending of the masculine and feminine poles within the individual, and full equality between man and women in the objective world. This is the unifying theme of all the Bible allegories, myths and parables, as well as the ancient Mysteries whereon Masonry was originally founded.

The Three Degrees of Mystical Ascent.

Entered Apprentice - Alchemical process of calcination.

The first stage involves refining your gross sense nature, killing your desire for material attractions and developing indifference to the lure of the outer world. It is all about subduing your lower passions, developing spiritual virtues and letting go of the past. It's about renewal and rebirth and new beginnings In Christianity. It is the same purifying process as repentance and water baptism. This Degree is represented by the pillar Boaz, (feminine, passive, receptive.) It is the way of the heart.

Fellow Craft - Alchemical process of dissolution.

The second stage involves clarifying your mind, until it becomes pure and strong enough to respond to the Light and wisdom of higher consciousness. This vision is followed by a desire to wipe from your life all obstacles to complete union with God. In Christianity, this stage is equivalent to receiving the baptism of the Holy Spirit, and having your mind renewed. This Degree is represented by the pillar Jachin, (male, active, regenerative.) It is the way of the head.

Master Mason - Alchemical process of separation.

The third stage, (the last and greatest trial,) involves the voluntary death of your sense of separation from the universal mind. As your limited personal ego dies, you become conscious of the omnipresence of God illuminating everything. It is complete union between the masculine head and feminine heart.

The raising in the Master Mason Degree can be seen as a separation of that which is eternal in man, from that which is merely temporary. In Christianity, it is the mystical death of the outer man and the resurrection of the inner man. The state you achieve as an initiate is also known as Cosmic Consciousness, which does not belong to any one religion. This Degree is represented by the Blazing Star, (Divine Spark). It is the stage of Gnosis.

The Great Work of Soul Illumination

The Great work is about developing an awakened Soul, - an illumined Soul which serves as a vehicle from the physical plane to higher celestial abodes. According to the ancient mystery schools, (Babylonian, Egyptian, Greece and Rome), unless a person develops a Soul in this life, the next life will be a void, nothing but waisted energy to be recycled once again.

And so, every Initiate must first learn, there is no purpose for their human incarnation than to develop an immortal Soul, which in the ancient time of the Egyptian Mysteries was depicted as a winged sun disk.

Spirit

Soul - Subconscious Mind

The Viel of Death

Brain - Conscious Mind

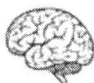

Body

The conscious mind is the house of the human brain. The subconscious is the house of the inner Soul. Unless the Soul is awakened the subconscious self with all its impressions, must at death pass into the unknown as an unconscious entity.

When the physical body dies, the brain (your personal story), also ceases to exist. The individualized Soul essence hidden within the subconscious mind, is the only part of us that will ascend heavenward.

The mind/brain is mortal just like the body and at the moment of death it passes into limbo and is forgotten. Only the subconscious mind – the unconscious Soul with its many impressions and experiences continues to carry on until it finds another incarnation. As we activate our subconscious through conscious effort, (the great work) our subconscious begins to give way to the awakening Soul, and if the process continues the Soul begins to develop into an awakened Illuminated entity. This is called the second birth in the bible. John 3:3

Every Masonic Initiate must make conscious effort to regenerate and rejuvenate his or her entire being. As they more and more come into the habit of meditative absorption through ritual work and loving service towards their fellowman, they will gradually arouse the Divine Spark which has so long been lying dormant within. The Spark will then ultimately burst forth into a Flame and become the Light of the Soul.

The life we live here and now, rather it be material or selfish or spiritual and noble, determines the degree of Light within us and whether this Light daily grows brighter or dimmer. As the mind become enlightened and rises above the life of mere mortal exitance, it gives birth to noble thoughts and holy virtues. These in turn electrify the Divine Spark essence within us, to such intensity as to burn up our past memories and negative karma, transforming our internal darkness into light and ultimately the new creation of an Illumined Soul.

To experience spiritual Regeneration and attain Immortality we must awaken the dormant sleeping Soul within. We do this through the science of Initiation. Therefore, until the Initiate comes to "know" his own Soul essence as the true Self. When the Soul becomes Illumined (Conscious of its Immortality) man in truth becomes the Temple of Light. This is the true purpose of all mystery schools, there is no other reason for their existence.

Within Freemasonry and the ancient mystery schools, our curriculum reveals that we are dual beings, part spiritual and part physical. Our single purpose is to bring our Divine Spark, our real eternal Self buried within our physical mortal self, into Soul consciousness. This is our only purpose for being here in the world of form. In the language of the Great Work, the process of cutting and polishing is called transmutation. Spiritual transmutation is changing the weakness of the physical mortal self into the divine virtues of the immortal Soul.

Simply put, transmutation is the replacement or substitution of our negative thoughts and emotions with the higher ones of God. The cultivation of such higher thoughts and feelings is essential for the development of the Divine Soul Spark within us. Until these higher qualities are activated in our everyday life, the higher worlds or God planes cannot be contacted. And this is the purpose of true spiritual Initiation and practice.

The Great Work and the Inner Temple

All energy is sexual, and when Raised to the head, it then becomes an Illumined Soul. This is why the first degree tells us to subdue our passions. Thus, one of the signs of a Master builder is that he or she practices sexual purity. If Initiation is followed through correctly and the candidate whole heartedly inters the path fasting and praying, then the kundalini serpent energy of the sleeping Soul essence will awaken within him and rise up to shine like a thousand suns in his forehead. Lighting flashes will strike within his forehead and the student will then know he has been sealed by the Light Divine.

Also, the temple of God which is not made with hands is directly related to the Alchemical work of Initiation, and clearly refers to spiritual development and progress of the Soul. The initiate himself is the Cornerstone of the Temple, it is the immortal Soul, the Christ within, the Philosopher's Stone, which is a new created identity from a rough to a perfect ashlar.

Stone is virtually eternal as a substance, as well as stable and strong. It symbolizes the true Soul: Man (the Son) when he realizes that he is truly ONE with God (the Father). That is the philosophers Stone that is the completion of the great work of alchemy; which transforms ordinary metals into GOLD. It is the Stone the builders (man or so-called masons in general) rejected; the chief cornerstone or foundation Stone of the temple.

The rough ashlar represents the Initiate now being cut out from the collective mass of sleeping humanity. He has not yet taken the form of perfection in the alchemical laboratory. Developing a perfect ashlar – an illumined Soul – requires chipping away the unnecessary stone with repeated effort until is a work of perfection. It is a process of removing our unconscious blocks to spiritual vision.

ROUGH ASHLER   PERFECT ASHLER

Subsequently, the candidate must pass through three symbolic degrees that he may attain this state of spiritual consciousness. To transform the rough ashlar of human perception into the perfect ashlar of spiritual consciousness requires certain tools as illustrated in the diagrams on the following pages. Make no mistake about it, this the Great Work of every Mystic Mason.

The Working Tools of an Entered Apprentice

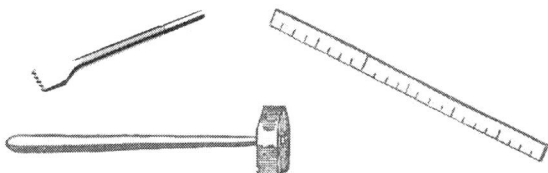

The Mallet, the Chisel, and the Twenty-Four-inch Gauge

The meaning of the working tools of an E.A. represents the application of the universal law of polarity and gender. All of nature has two poles of manifestation that is represented by the Mallet (the active principle) and the Chisel (the passive). Likewise, since all is mind and the mind has the same two corresponding poles (masculine and feminine) the tools are symbolic then of a mental process that seeks to attain balance though a third force of equilibrium, which is the balanced, androgynous, principle.

The Mallet represents the force of active intelligence and divine will. It is what decrees a thing and makes it so. Without this force nothing can be achieved. The Chisel receives its power from the gravel the same as the (passive) subconscious receives its directions from the conscious (active) mind. The twenty-four-inch Gauge represents the neutralizing balance. Twenty-four divisible by three comes to 888, which is numerally the name of "Jesus Christ" or Messiah in Hebrew gematria. The significance meaning that one attains Christ consciousness who finds equilibrium.

The Working Tools of a Fellow Craft

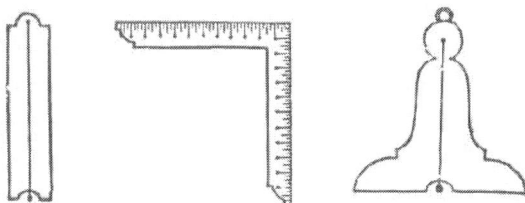

The Level the Square and the Plumb

The three Tools of an FC are tools of analyzation, symbolizing contemplative meditation, while the three tools of an EA are tools of force. These are two different mind states, as the EA engages in mostly ordinary thought processes.

The Level establishes horizontals, and thus symbolizes passive energy, which is feminine (the horizontal is a line "at rest"). Furthermore, the shape of the level resembles a female's breast (feminine energy). The Plumb establishes perpendicular lines and thus symbolizes active energy, which is masculine (the perpendicular or vertical line is an upright line, representing activity). The shape of the plumb resembles a male's erect penis (masculine energy).

The level is in the west of the lodge, which is the place of sunset, emblematic of passive force (the sun at its lowest point). The plumb is in the south, which is the place of the sun's highest elevation, and is thus emblematic of active force. The square is a horizontal and perpendicular united and thus symbolizes neutral or balanced energy; or androgynous energy (male and female at the same time; or neither male nor female). The square is in the East, which is the balance or middle point between the south and west in regards to the 3 main points of the sun's daily journey through heaven.

The Working Tools of a Master Mason

The Compass, Trowel, and Setting Maul

The Compass, Trowel, and Setting Maul together symbolize that a Master Mason is Omnipresent (Compass or Circle); Omniscient (Trowel; as the trowel is the SPIRITUAL EYE of a literal Mason in literal masonry); and Omnipotent (Setting Maul). In other words, a Master Mason is completely God Realized. This is why a Master Mason can sit wherever he wants in the Lodge (with the exception of officer's stations), while EA's must sit in the North (Darkness) and FC's in the South (Light).

Those tools as trinities represent different manifestations or levels of the active, passive, and neutral manifestations of Mind/God/Consciousness. But we must apply them to the rough ashlar and perfect ashlar along with the tools, as the tools (trinity of mind energy) are used to shape the Stone (mind or Soul). It is mind acting upon mind; or the mind working upon itself to transform itself into the perfect stone or philosophers Stone.

So, combining the tools of all 3 degrees produces 3x3, which is 9, symbolizing self completion, or God Consciousness, as each part of the trinity of Energy (Active, Passive, Neutral) contains within it the other two parts, giving you three times three = 9.

The number 3 represents union between the numbers 1 and 2. Mathematically, 1 and 2 give birth to the number 3. The number 3 is also allegorized within the three stages of death, burial and resurrection. Man is a tripartite being- body, mind and spirit. There are only three stages of life- youth, adulthood and old age. There are only three states of consciousness- conscious, subconscious, and superconscious. And there are only three stages of spiritual transformation- purification, illumination and union.

The number 3 also forms a perfect triangle- active, passive and neutral. The Ancient Egyptian ceremony of Initiation led the candidate to a door shaped exactly as a Masonic apron- a triangle over a square, symbolizing his progression from an earthly, material existence, (square,) into a heavenly, spiritual existence of higher learning, (triangle.) Based on this model, the ancient Sages and mystics of Masonry established a three-step program to reach enlightenment. This is why there are only three Degrees of Initiation. The highest rank anyone can achieve is Master Mason. The side Degrees of the Scottish and York rites are only for the purpose of going deeper into the experiential knowledge of the three blue Degrees.

The triangle is a symbol of perfection. The law of duality, being a universal law, is represented by two points of the triangle. When two different forces of nature are brought together, a third condition or creation arises at the point where they will be brought together. That third point or point of equilibrium is the state of wholeness. - The Eye is symbolical of spiritual vision which activates God realization. When the Eye was adopted as the symbol of the Supreme Ruler of the Universe, it was intended to typify the all-inclusive mind of God which sees all, and therefore knows all. In this sense the Eye came to be the symbol of Divine Consciousness or Cosmic Consciousness. Thus, the combination of the two symbols as we have them above alludes to the perfection of the Divine consciousness, its completeness, wholeness and spiritual at-one-ment.

The Temple of Initiation

Every Masonic temple symbolically represents the tabernacle of the Hebrews, which was constructed to reveal these same Degrees of Initiation that are based on the law of three. The tabernacle was merely a temple patterned after the temples of Egypt. Every part of the tabernacle was symbolic of some great spiritual truth. To the ignorant masses it was but a place in which to bring offerings and to make a sacrifice; to the wise it was a temple of learning, sacred to the universal wisdom.

The Outer Court represents the first stage of purification, corresponding to the outer physical level of experience involving the discipline and control of the objective sense. **The Holy Place** represents the second stage of Illumination, corresponding to the inner psychological level of experience involving the discipline of the subjective mental nature. **The Holy of Holies** represents Divine revelation, corresponding to the mystical level of spiritual perfection. This is the stage of mystical death and resurrection, where you are raised above the mortal plane and become a Master Adept.

In the hermetic teachings of, "The Kybalion by the Three Initiates," there are three great planes of existence. They subsequently correspond to the three Degrees of Freemasonry, and also Christied mysticism, whereby every initiate ascends towards greater and greater Light through inner work. 1. The Great Physical Plane. 2. The Great Mental Plane. 3. The Great Spiritual Plane.

Even in the Bible, Solomon's Temple was a perfect blueprint for this same threefold process of mystical ascent. Solomon's temple comprises three floors, each of which are allegorically played out in every Masonic Initiation.

The Ground Floor.
The Middle Chamber.
The Sanctum Sanctorum.

Allegorically these three levels of the temple refer to the threefold nature of man as the body, (ground floor,) mind, (middle chamber,) and Spirit, (the Sanctum Santorum). This is why some Christied mystics also become Freemasons. It is in order to experience the three Degrees, as modern-day Masonry has a perfect alchemical system of Initiation according to this Divine plan.

1st Degree, The Physical Nature of Man.
2nd Degree, The Mental Nature of Man.
3rd Degree, The Spiritual Nature of Man.

The most ancient Mysteries were always divided into the lesser and the greater- the former being intended only to awaken curiosity, to test the character of the candidate, and, (by symbolic purifications,) to prepare him for his introduction into the greater Mysteries of Divine Gnosis.

The narrow way to King Solomon's temple was between two pillars that adorned the porch, and between which every candidate had to pass as he journeyed towards the spiritual Light. These two pillars have been part of every mystery temple the world has ever known. They have been known as the pillars of the Sun and Moon, and of Fire and Water.

In Masonry the twin columns are known as the two pillars of Jachin and Boaz. Jachin represents the masculine pole or the head- the center of reason. Boaz symbolizes the feminine or the heart- the center of love. When these two poles are brought into equilibrium, reason will be ruled by love and love will be stabilized by reason.

The wisdom of the ancient mystics tells us, "enlightenment occurs only after the mind falls into the heart," and this is exactly what is alluded to in the first three Degrees of freemasonry. Before there can be any true lasting peace, we must have our minds filled with Christ Light and our hearts radiant with Christ Love. Only then are we truly born again.

As we have already discussed above, the Masonic Lodge is an alchemical laboratory, where the candidate goes through three stages of Initiation and Regeneration. The Lodge itself is a layout of Solomon's temple. That Temple has three principal divisions: the outer court, the inner court, and the Holy of Holies. Members of the first, (Entered Apprentice,) Degree meet on the outer court. The second, (Fellow Craft,) Degree assembles within the inner court. Those of the third, (Master,) Degree join together within the Holy of Holies. Symbolically speaking, the outer court represents the lower mind, the inner court is the higher mind, and the spiritual world is the Holy of Holies- which is the kingdom of heaven within you that Christ proclaimed.

Tabernacle of Moses

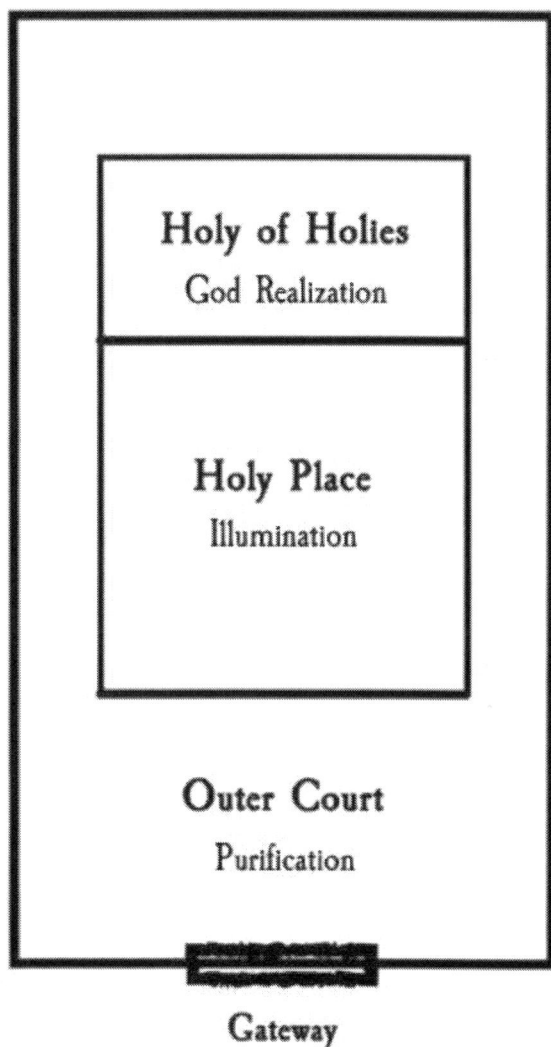

Holy of Holies
God Realization

Holy Place
Illumination

Outer Court
Purification

Gateway

You Are the Temple of God. (Body, Mind, Spirit) To enter the Temple is to enter into yourself and discover the Most Holy Place within you. These three levels can also be seen as the conscious, subconscious and superconscious states of mind.

The Masonic Quest

The term "Mason" is derived from "PHREE MESSEN", which is an Egyptian term meaning "Children of Light." The key ideal of Mystic Masonry is Self-Realization by means of Initiation. The Craft was founded upon three fundamental Degrees. These are Entered Apprentice, Fellow Craft, and Master Mason. The inner attainments are purification, illumination, and Self Mastery.

The candidate was first called an aspirant, or seeker of the truth, and the initial ceremony which he underwent was a purification by water. In this condition, he may be compared to the Entered Apprentice of the Masonic rites, as all the ceremonies in the first Degree of Masonry are symbolic of an internal purification.

In the lesser Mysteries, the candidate took an oath of secrecy followed by preparatory instruction, which enabled him to understand the developments of higher learning. He was now called an Initiate, and may be compared to the Fellow Craft of Freemasonry. In the greater Mysteries, the whole knowledge of the Divine truths- which was the object of Initiation- was communicated. Here we find the ceremonies of mystical death and resurrection. At this stage, the candidate may correctly be called a Master Mason.

In the image to the right; the initiate stands blindfolded between the two columns of his fiery (conscious,) and watery (unconscious,) mind. His eyes are blinded from the outer world as he turns within himself. When the two pillars are spiritually activated through Initiation the blinders come off, and a new spiritual vision is revealed. Only then is he born again.

The Alchemy of Soul Illumination
This image represents the middle path of Illumination.
The Illumined Soul always stands between two allegorical Pillars.
There is no enlightenment without meditative equilibrium.

The Masonic Origin of all Religions

Thus far we have seen that Freemasonry is an alchemical school for spiritual enlightenment. And that alchemy is not something you do; it is something you are. For example, all energy is sexual, meaning that the entire universe is composed of male (active) and female (receptive) energy. One could say nothing is really happening apart from the dance between these two polarities. The union between the left and right hemispheres of our psychology that when balanced gives birth to the Illumined Soul.

The law of polarity is one of the main secrets revealed within all the ancient mystery schools. This law is in operation within every man and women in the universe. The goal of Freemasonry is "to make good men better" which is to merge one's higher self with Deity. When the lower is submitted to the higher, the higher is submitted to God. This is the great work and it is exactly what the three Degrees of Masonry are really about.

Ancient Masonry is symbolic of an inner spiritual reality, it is a universal allegory, the true religion of all mankind. Masonry is a decedent of a divinely imparted religion which predates the dates attributed to Solomon's temple in the bible.

Masonry and its allegorical rituals, and its symbols and numbers are all that remains to us of the very first religion of antiquity so old that it is impossible to fix a date. It was the first unified world religion. Then came the era of separation (confusion or babel) of the many differing religions. All religions today have the same essential principles that where carried over from the most ancient world religion.

All religions came from ancient Masonry and are offshoots of its wisdom. The Initiation, death and resurrection of everyone who seeks the Light is the oldest ritual and most ancient myth in all of history. The creed of ancient Masonry had only two principles that sum up everything we need to know, and all lesser dogmas and doctrines sum up these two fundamental truths.

First, that GOD IS, the Universal Mind that governs maintains and sustains all creation by the living word of mental vibration and the Light of cosmic law. Secondly, we are an expression of that Light, immortal just like our Source, yet wandering in the darkness or mortal fear and false perception. Eventually we must each find our way back from whence we came. We must travel to the East by way of the north and the Light will reveal itself to us. We must learn to subdue our passions, attune to our Spirit, until finally we will pass through the portal of death and enter into eternal life as a fully Illumined Soul.

Faith in God and belief in Immortality- this is the theme and creed of ancient Masonry, which all its symbols, rituals and secrets bear witness. There is not a single religion under heaven that did not evolve from these same universal truths. Masonry is the source of all the world's religions. From Atlantis to Egypt, to Greece. I am speaking of ancient Masonry as the world's first religion and not modern Masonry.

The Masonic Path of Christ Consciousness

To discover Christianity's deeper mysteries of esoteric wisdom, we need only to look at the symbol of Christ crucified between two thieves, both with opposite natures, with Christ in the center. This is an allusion to the three pillars of alchemy- body, mind, and spirit, which must be crucified through the process of Initiation, for the new being to emerge.

The alchemical number 3 represents the union of polar opposites (the two thieves) which are experienced in the 1st and 2nd Degree- symbolized by the two pillars in the temple. Our true Self is seen as the 3rd pillar at the center, who is spiritually risen in the 3rd Degree. As seen in nature the union of opposites (masculine and feminine,) gives birth to a third force. This rule of three is seen everywhere in Masonic and Christian symbolism, as well as in the world of biology. It is symbolic of spiritual perfection. It completes the triangle and is the final Degree in the alchemical laboratory of blue Lodge Masonry.

According to esoteric Christianity, the crucifixion is a parable, an allegory that describes the process of Initiation. There are two thieves hanging on each side of the crucified Christ. The crucified Christ in you, also hangs between these same allegorical thieves. In Masonry these thieves are the two pillars of the Lodge, which are symbolic of the body and mind. When they are undisciplined and left to their own delusions, they become thieves, robbing us of our own Christhood, which is crucified on the cross of matter.

Freemasonry, just like the Christic mysteries, deals with the tripartite nature of man, physical, mental, spiritual, (in that order,) by means of the three Degrees. The purification of our physical actions and mental thoughts leads us to the final stage of enlightenment. This is the way of Initiation in all mystery schools.

The Crucifixion takes place on the cross of our human experience. Christ, (which is our true spiritual will,) is crucified between the two thieves of our fallen physical and mental natures. According to the mysteries; they must all three be crucified before any resurrection is possible. **To the body we decree, "I need do nothing". To the mind we say "Be still and know". And to our will we let go and say "Not my will but thine will be done".**

The Christian cross represents the point of intersection between the earthly (horizontal) and heavenly (vertical) planes of experience. The Initiatic Path of the cross symbolizes the path of the kundalini fire as it rises from the base of the spine to the head. The Christ on the cross signifies the Spirit within man whose ultimate goal is to become a fully Christed one. Everyone born into the world is a crucified Christ on the cross of mortal existence, until they are resurrected by the spiritual birth of their true Divine nature.

Another Masonic interpretation is that the two thieves represent the unenlightened condition of mankind. They are identified with the first two Degrees of Masonic Initiation. The thief on the left represents our fallen physical nature that clings to bodily survival. The other thief is our fallen mental nature, which desires only to be in heaven with Christ today. When these two thieves, (our fallen physical and mental natures,) are crucified and Christed through the process of Initiation, the eternal Christ in you is taken off the cross, were he resurrects from the empty tomb of mortal existence.

Christs ascent into "Heaven" is another concept of the kundalini rising to the crown chakra. Heaven, Earth, and Hell are all concepts which preceded from older religions. Heaven is symbolic of the seventh chakra, also known as the "crown chakra." The earth or "middle kingdom" is symbolic of the heart chakra and "Hell" symbolizes the base chakra, where the hot fiery serpent kundalini lies dormant and must be set free.

Neither Christianity of to-day nor modern Freemasonry is the direct decedent of the Greater Mysteries, but are mere remnants of the Supreme Wisdom of Antiquity. Modern Freemasonry and modern Christianity are merely offshoots of the ancient mystery religion. In fact, many in modern Masonry and modern Christianity are completely ignorant of their true origins and will reject any connection with the secret doctrines of Antiquity.

Mystic Masonry is the home of the mysteries and the seat of Initiation. Masonic rituals dramatize the Light within as it evolves from stage to stage. Essentially, being a Mason is a state of enlightened Being. 'Being a Mason' does not simply mean going to a social Lodge and participating in community service. It is a spiritual state of consciousness, a "Revelation of Light" which invokes the will, illumines the mind and enlightens the heart. It is a perfect path to enlightenment.

Christ (our immortal Self) is crucified in equilibrium between the two extremes of our lower and higher natures. The lower mind does not repent, but the higher recognizes the Christ and is promised eternal life. According to the mysteries; the lower mind is the instrument of habit, worldly appetites, and self-preservation. The higher mind is intuitive and receives the Light of spiritual vision. It is only the higher mind which can be lifted up into the world of Divine truth, as all the holy mysteries and symbols reveal.

The Secret Doctrine of Christ.

It may come as a surprise to many Christians that the biblical Jesus did in fact, have a secret doctrine. If anyone doubts that Jesus transmitted his esoteric mysteries only to an elect few, then they must read these scriptures below. Just like in the Masonic mystery schools, Jesus was attempting to protect the deepest mysteries of the kingdom from the profane masses who proved themselves unworthy of his deeper teachings. "But without a parable spake he not unto them: and when they were alone, he expounded all things to his (Initiated) disciples," Mark 4:34 "And he charged them that they should tell no man of him." Mark 8:30 - Again: "Give not that which is holy unto the dogs, neither cast ye your pearls before swine, lest they trample them under their feet, and turn again and rend you." Matt 7:6 And again "To you it has been granted to know the inner mysteries of the kingdom, but to them without, it has not been given," Matt 13:11

The true teachings of the Bible are allegorical. (read Manly P. Halls book, "How to interpret your Bible). One could even say, the entire Bible is a Freemasonic manual based on Qabalah, that clearly points out, that the allegorical Jesus was the Grand Master or high priest after the order of Melchizedek, which are all Masonic terms describing the Initiatic process. Jesus, to the early Christians, was the symbolic Hierophant of the Mystic Body of a Heavenly Lodge, called the Church.

Christianity today is just the remaining remnant of what was once a powerhouse mystery school for enlightenment. Neither Christianity of today nor modern Freemasonry seems to remember the Greater Mysteries from which they were first conceived.

The scriptures are also full of allegorical references to ancient Masonry and building with stone. Jesus himself is described as a carpenter, but a truer meaning is a Master builder. Jesus says, "The stone which the builders rejected is become the head of the corner," Mark 12:10. Also in John 1:42, Jesus makes Simon Peter a stone, a foundation stone of a spiritual temple. The living temple, is the body of Christ, (the true Church,) which is a temple not made with hands, but with spiritual and moral character. The Freemasons likewise labor on the construction of this same spiritual temple, and not a physical one. As did the early Christians and every other true spiritual tradition.

The deeper mysteries of Jesus's building analogies relate to the rite of spiritual resurrection. Jesus even portrays himself as a temple builder. He said, "Destroy this temple, and in three days I will raise it up." In this passage Jesus was alluding to the resurrected life in the Spirit. He knew that he would triumph over his initiatory death he was to undergo, the same as every Freemason in every Lodge today. He also viewed the process in terms of spiritual rebuilding. Christ being "the Chief Corner Stone," and each mystic Mason a "living stone."

The goal of all Initiatic processes is the purification of the natural human being; that is, the extraction of the pure gold of our spiritual essence from the husk of the outer personality. The final objective is the purification of our distorted perceptions and the realization of an elevated state of consciousness, wherein consciousness enters into a union with the higher mind and ultimately with the Universal Mind. For it is written, "Equilibrium is the basis of the Great Work" When the astral cord (the etheric body) is cut from all worldly attachments, the Spirit in you is resurrected to newness of life. Only those who experience this state of Illumination are called "twice born" or "born again.

The compass and the square, represent our heavenly
(spiritual nature) and earthly (human nature). When
these two forces find equilibrium, the lamp of spiritual
vision illuminates our inner Soul. In Freemasonry there
is a letter G in the middle of the square and compass,
symbolizing the Divine Spark or God within. – as
Plato declared, "May the inner man and the outer man
become one." And by 'the inside and the outside' he
means this- that the inside is the Soul and the outside
is the body. When the inner consciousness governs the
outer picture of things then the Masonic square and
Compass have overlapped and become one.

Part 3

Qabalah and Freemasonry

The study of Qabalah is why many of us seekers on the path expand beyond our own radical Christian beliefs and become Freemasons, in search for more Light. What I discovered is that Freemasonry, in its essence, is derived from Qabalah as part of the great wisdom traditions. In fact, all middle eastern religions came from Qabalah, including Christianity, and all their doctrines can be found within it, even with the Eastern Religions, (Buddhism and Hinduism,) which see the Creator and the Creation as Divine emanations- "The Great Chain of Being." Likewise, the mystery school of Freemasonry is a search after the same transcendental Light, which leads us directly back to the Qabalah, as all religions originated from Qabalah and all must eventually return to it.

The word Qabalah means, "to receive," or, "that which is constantly being received." What is being received? The flow of energy in the universe– of waves, sounds and vibrations of spiritual Light– all in different frequencies, levels and proportions. Along with this energy are impulses, insights and impressions in thoughts, images, feelings, prophetic word and angelic revelations. The ultimate reception is Divine Illumination- the experience of being in communion with all that is- the Absolute- the Creator- receiving Divine inspiration- and unlocking the passions of the Soul.

The Star of Solomon relates to the union of opposites on the tree of life. It references the union of the spiritual and physical, with spiritual reality reaching down and physical reality stretching upward. This intertwining of worlds can be seen as a representation of the Hermetic principle, "As above, so below." As Jesus also said, "On earth as it is in heaven". It references how changes in one world reflect changes in the other. If we look closely, we can see a cube in the center of the star, representing the Perfect Ashlar, or Philosopher's Stone.

Solomon's Star is made of two interlocking triangles. The symbol also dates back to the ancient Hindu traditions, which symbolizes both God and mankind. The Triangle is symbolic of the Trinity, the Father, the Son and Manifestation. The triangle pointing down represents God reaching down to man, and the triangle pointing up represent man reaching up to God. So in this symbol they are united – they have become One. Thus, this symbol always represents complete union with God and humanity. It is identical to the mystic union of the Masonic Square and Compass, the merging of the elements fire and water.

To the Qabalist, similar to the Freemasons, the reconciliation of opposites is viewed as a three-fold process. First the opposites are viewed as separate and indifferent to each other. In the second stage of development, the opposites become aware of their differences and resistance and conflict result.

These two stages can be symbolized by the myth of
Adam and Eve in the Garden. At first, they were
ignorant of their differences until they ate of the tree of
knowledge and then realized they were naked and
noticed their differences in sexuality. The third and final
stage in the reconciliation of opposites is one of
harmony. Each one is still distinct but of equal weight,
blending together and cooperating together in mutual
love. For example, in the judicial system of ancient
Israel, justice was always balanced with mercy. And
then again in the new covenant gospels, it is seen as
the equilibrium between the seeming opposites of law
and grace.

The Secret Name of God

יהוה

According the Qabalistic tradition, the name of God,
or Lost Word of Freemasonry, is only spoken by
"lettering it "or spelling it out, "having it" receiving
and cutting it in half, or substituting it, (using a
substitute name or word).

The reason for this custom, is that the true pronunciation of this name or word was lost, due to the destruction of king Solomon's temple. Thus, the name or "Word" is called the "Lost Word" in the Qabalistic tradition. This same tradition informs us that the true pronunciation of the Lost Word was known only by the Initiated Higher Priest of the Hebrew Temple, who would utter in only one day a year. This day is called "Yon Kippur", meaning the Day of At-one-ment. The Lost word was only spoken in a whisper, or in "low breath", in the Holy of Holies, which housed the Ark of the covenant.

By having the Lost Word. One discovers that it conceals the Hermetic Principle of Gender, which teaches us that the God of the Universe, is both Male and Female. This also reveals to us that the physical universe is God's reflection made visible.

He הוי

She יהו

The two words above are "Hu" and Heey", meaning "He and "She". These are symbolized by the square and compass in Freemasonry, and throughout all the Degrees of Initiation. In fact, the entire Biblical story as represented in the Qabalah, is an allegory for Initiation. The Temple we must all enter, is the inward journey of the Initiate, and the Holy of Holies represents the most Holy Place within oneself. The NAME of God is the union of the masculine and feminine qualities of the candidate, balance between the head and heart or reason and intuition. It is realized or 'Spoken" only on the day of At-one-ment, because that is the moment of Mystic Union with the God Self within.

By writing the Lost Word vertically, one discovers that it conceals the Hermetic Principle of correspondence, which teaches us that the human Being is the Universe, or God in miniature, or God Incarnated in the flesh "And the Word became flesh and dwelt among us, and we beheld His glory, the glory as of the only begotten of the Father, full of grace and truth." John 1:14

The three Qabalistic pillars are also the same as Ida, Shushumna and Pingala in the Yoga system of ancient India. Sushumna is the channel of ascent of kundalini, placed between the Solar and Lunar qualities of Pingala and Ida. The three pillars may also be likened to Yin and Yang, the female and male principles of Taoism, with the Tao, (the way,) as the middle pillar. Qabalists, however, see the left and right pillars as positive, (active,) and negative, (passive,) phases of manifestation. The middle pillar is consciousness itself.

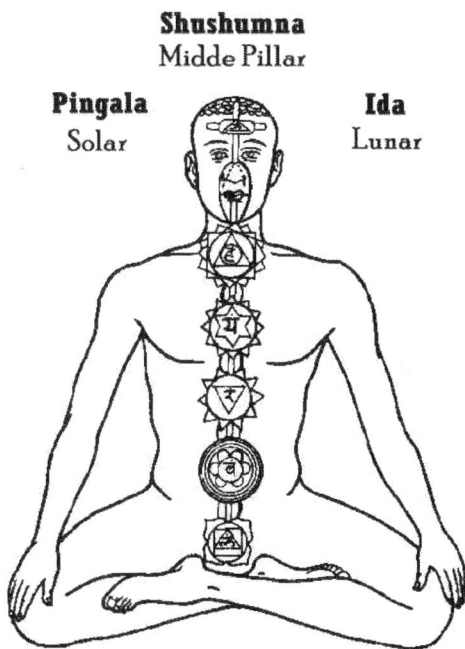

Shushumna
Midde Pillar

Pingala   **Ida**
Solar   Lunar

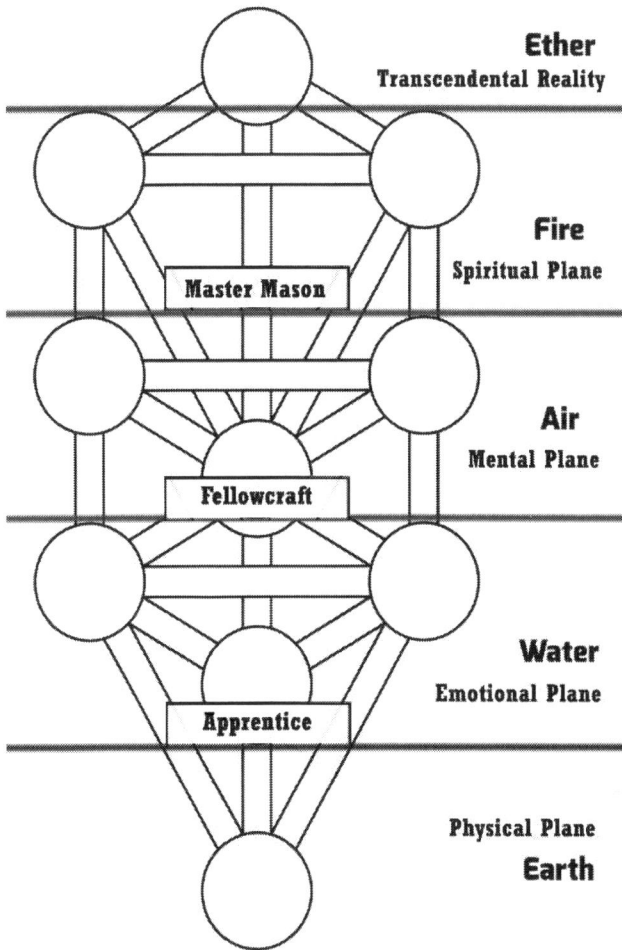

Ether
Transcendental Reality

Fire
Spiritual Plane

Master Mason

Air
Mental Plane

Fellowcraft

Water
Emotional Plane

Apprentice

Physical Plane
Earth

The way of Masonic Initiation, as revealed on the tree of life, is an upward ascension through the various elemental planes of creation. Each plane is encoded and revealed in the Bible as the sacred name of God-YHWH. Each letter of God's name stands for the elements of nature within the four worlds of Qabalah. The five-pointed star, or pentagram, also contains the same symbolic meaning.

From an Initiation standpoint, the initiate in the Gnostic mystery schools would go through various levels of Qabalistic baptism. They progressed upwards in advancement on the tree of life, moving closer to the Source of Deity, one Degree at a time. The first stage was a baptism by water, the second a baptism by air, and the last a baptism by fire, progressing from the gross to the subtlest element. In the three Degrees of Freemasonry, the alchemical process of an element always goes from earth to water, from water to air and from air to fire. It may even come as a surprise to many Masons that the alchemical process is symbolically alluded to in the penalties of their obligation. In the penalty of the first-Degree, the element of water is alluded to. The second-Degree penalty alludes to air. The third-Degree, fire.

Fire

3rd Degree

Air

2nd Degree

Water

1st Degree

Earth

I (Yod)

H (He)

V (Vau)

H (He)

All stages of spiritual alchemy are about breaking down various base parts of one's character that stand in the way of Illumination. The same use of the elements is also found in the ancient mystery schools of Egypt, as well as the early Gnostic schools of Christ followers. The new Initiate went through the three baptisms of water, air, and finally the baptism of the Holy Ghost and fire.

Each person must quest inward and upward for Initiation into the higher levels of consciousness, represented by water, air, and fire. As Jesus said, "Those who came before me baptized with the element of water, but I have come to baptize with the element of fire." In other words, Jesus taught mystical union with the Divine will, through the alchemical fire of Spirit baptism. By using the layout on the cosmic tree, the initiate actually must move up and past each of these levels as he moves closer to the upper Divine realms. He is attempting to achieve mystical union with Deity after having experienced a fall into matter.

The Qabalah focuses on studying the structure of the four creative worlds as they evolve from above down to our world. Our purpose is to prepare our vessel, and open our hearts to experience the spiritual world and the Creator. There really is no other revelation of the Creator to man than what is revealed in the mystical Qabalah. A seeker of truth can feel the Illumination of Divine Light only by changing his state of consciousness inwardly and ascending upward on the cosmic tree of life, also called 'Jacob's ladder'.

The entire Initiatic process is a journey through the three higher worlds: astral, mental, and spiritual. Every mystery school goes by this map of creation. Everyone enters the Lodge from the material plane. In the first-Degree we are Initiated into the astral plane. In the second-Degree we are purified on the mental plane, and in the third-Degree, we are spiritually reborn. There is no other way of salvation, as Christ so proclaimed, "You must be born from above the earthly plane." This subject we will discuss in depth in the next chapter, suffice it to say that a true Initiation is always through all the elements, as seen in Freemasonry and represented by the three upper worlds of Qabalah.

This is the true meaning of esoteric spirituality, as Light descends from the Creator, building four planes on its way down through the elements of Fire, Air, Water, and finally Earth. These Degrees are not perceived outwardly, but are inside of ourselves. They are Degrees of internal spiritual transformation. When we change something inside us, we ascend by one Degree. When we change another, we climb another Degree and so on. As the Bible says, "from glory to glory." This is the purpose of our Initiatic experience.

Ascent of the Ladder of Perfection

In the esoteric mystery schools, the ladder was a symbol of moral and spiritual progress, symbolic of the Soul's approach to perfection. Each rung of the ladder represents higher levels of consciousness, as we ascend upward through the higher worlds on the Qabalistic tree of life. The sleeping man at the bottom of the ladder is our unconscious sleep state in the human condition, who must yet awaken from the mortal dream, advancing by Degrees- from earth to heaven- from death to life- from human to Divine.

Welcome to the path of Illumination.

Amor Russell

Printed in Great Britain
by Amazon